THE CALENDAR AND LECTIONARY:

A Reconsideration

THE CALENDAR
AND
LECTIONARY

A Reconsideration

BY
THE JOINT LITURGICAL GROUP

Edited by
Ronald C. D. Jasper

London
OXFORD UNIVERSITY PRESS
NEW YORK TORONTO
1967

Oxford University Press, Ely House, London W.1

GLASGOW NEW YORK TORONTO MELBOURNE WELLINGTON
CAPE TOWN SALISBURY IBADAN NAIROBI LUSAKA ADDIS ABABA
BOMBAY CALCUTTA MADRAS KARACHI LAHORE DACCA
KUALA LUMPUR HONG KONG TOKYO

PRINTED IN GREAT BRITAIN BY
WESTERN PRINTING SERVICES LTD BRISTOL

CONTENTS

MEMBERS OF THE
JOINT LITURGICAL GROUP

1. *Church of England*

   The Dean of Bristol (The Very Revd. D. E. W. Harrison, M.A.), Chairman

   The Rt. Revd. H. de Candole, M.A. (sometime Bishop of Knaresborough)

   The Revd. Canon R. C. D. Jasper, M.A., D.D., F.R.Hist.S., Secretary

2. *Church of Scotland*

   The Revd. J. A. Lamb, M.A., Ph.D., D.D.

   F. N. Davidson Kelly Esq., LL.B., S.S.C.

3. *The Baptist Union of Great Britain and Ireland*

   The Revd. Neville Clark, M.A., S.T.M.

   The Revd. Stephen F. Winward, M.A., B.D.

4. *The Congregational Church of England and Wales*

   The Revd. J. M. Todd, M.A.

   The Revd. W. E. Evans, B.A., B.D.

5. *The Episcopal Church in Scotland*

   The Bishop of Glasgow, Primus (The Most Revd. F. H. Moncrieff, M.A.)

   The Revd. A. O. Barkway, M.A.

6. *The Methodist Church*

   The Revd. G. S. Wakefield, M.A., B.Litt.

   The Revd. A. Raymond George, M.A., B.D.

7. *The Presbyterian Church of England*
   The Revd. R. Aled Davies, M.A.
   The Revd. R. D. Whitehorn, M.A., D.D.

8. *The Churches of Christ*
   The Revd. W. G. Baker, M.A., S.T.M., D.D.

9. *Observer of the Church of Rome*
   The Revd. Canon R. Pilkington

STATEMENT

INFORMAL discussion on liturgical matters between interested people from various Churches in Great Britain have indicated that the time is now ripe for the creation of a Joint Liturgical Group which can develop given projects and questions of public worship. The Archbishop of Canterbury was asked to help bring such a Group into being by issuing invitations to the Churches concerned to appoint members. His Grace kindly agreed to do so and himself appointed the representatives of the Church of England, while those of other Churches have been appointed by their respective bodies.

At its first meeting on 10-11 October 1963 the Group elected the Dean of Bristol as its Chairman and Dr. Jasper as its Secretary.

It is clearly to be understood that any work produced by this Group will have no authority greater than that which its own members give to it by their own weight; but it will be for particular Churches, through their own customary modes of decision, to make use of the results if they are willing to do so.

The initial projects which the Group has decided to discuss are these:

1. The planning of a Calendar, Forms of Daily Service, and a Lectionary which the Churches might be glad to have in common.
2. The planning of joint forms of service which might be

used with the approval of the several Churches on occasions for united worship, such as the Week of Prayer for Unity and Holy Week.

3. The consideration of the structure of the service of Holy Communion.

INTRODUCTION

In presenting this work to the Churches for their consideration the Joint Liturgical Group hopes that it might be
regarded as a modest contribution towards a more realistic
understanding of the Church's year and a more effective use
of the Bible at the principal Sunday services.

The whole scheme is flexible. Some people might find the
Calendar proposals too radical; and yet at the same time they
might wish to use some, if not the whole, of the Lectionary.
They will find that the continued use of the traditional
names for the various Sundays and seasons of the year will
not prevent them from making the fullest possible use of the
new scheme of lessons. If necessary, the Lectionary for both
years can be used concurrently, the readings for the first year
being used, for example, in the morning and those for the
second year in the evening. Then, in the following year, the
second year readings might be used in the morning and the
first year readings in the evening. Again, only two of the
three readings need be used at one service: but it is greatly to
be hoped that the Controlling Lection should always be one
of them.

Obviously these proposals cannot stand entirely alone.
There are other needs to be met: and the Group wishes to
indicate three of these needs to which consideration is being
given.

1. The provision of suitable collects.
2. The observance of Holy Week.
3. The possible need for a further lectionary for use at

non-eucharistic services, and in which provision is made for many of the special Sundays and occasions which are observed by the various churches.

The Group wishes to emphasize that these proposals have no sort of official status; while the essays are the personal expositions of the proposals by the members under whose names they appear. It will now remain for the various Churches to consider all this material and to make use of it if they find it acceptable.

D. E. W. HARRISON,
Chairman

April 1966

THE CALENDAR

H. DE CANDOLE

THE Christian Church cannot ignore Time. For the Christian Gospel is not a system of ideas but the story of 'the saving deeds of the Lord'. It is right and natural therefore that these great acts should not only be recorded in Scripture, and summarized in the Creeds, but lived over again in the liturgical observances of the Christian Year. By it, recurring witness is given to the facts of the Gospel for the thankful remembrance of what Christ in His incarnate life wrought for the world. There is something more. For it enables the worshipping Church and the worshipping Christian to enter afresh into the meaning of these saving events or 'mysteries', and be renewed in their power.

The story of the emergence of the Christian Year is a long and fascinating one. Like all institutions, it requires from time to time a fresh look and possible reform. This essay attempts no more than a brief account of the outline of its history, in view of suggestions made below.

The Christian Calendar falls into two sections—the *Temporale* or Calendar of Time (i.e. the various seasons of the Christian Year), and the *Sanctorale*, or Holy Days, mainly those assigned to the commemoration of saints. The latter is for the most part a separate matter, and is not here under consideration. It was severely pruned by the Churches of the Reformation in the West, in some places removed almost entirely; though the Church of England retained both Red Letter (the principal) Days, consisting of feasts of apostles and other saints of the New Testament, and Black Letter Days without liturgical provision, commemorating lesser occasions and later saints. We are concerned here with the pastoral needs of ordinary congregations which consist overwhelmingly of Sunday worshippers only.

The *Temporale* supplies the Sundays of the Christian Year and those greater Holy Days, falling normally or sometimes on weekdays, which commemorate major events in our Lord's life, such as Christmas Day, Epiphany, Good Friday and Ascension Day. In many parts of Reformed Christendom these fell into disuse for a considerable time, but happily their restoration to fuller observance has been a marked feature of recent years.

Sabbath into Sunday

The use of regular occasions in the course of the year for special observance is familiar in most religions; and it was a characteristic of the Jewish religion, in which our Lord, his apostles, and the earliest Christians grew up. Thus it was at Passover time that the events of our Lord's crucifixion and resurrection took place, and at Pentecost that the Holy Spirit was given to the Church. These were therefore, from the very beginning, part of the framework of the Christian experience, and continued to be so. But from very early Christian days an observance arose, which was peculiarly their own. The Jewish Church had received the tradition, ordained as they claimed by God himself, to 'Keep holy the sabbath day', i.e. the seventh day, Saturday. The earliest Christians at Jerusalem appear to have continued this practice as would have been expected. But to this was added a special Christian observance of the first day of the week. (cf. Acts 20.7, 1 Corinthians 16.2). This was known as the Lord's day

(Revelation 1.10), and is our Sunday. Its observance may have started as early as the eighth day after the Resurrection (St. John 20.26). When the Church moved out from Palestine into the Gentile world, and made converts from non-Jewish races, it was not long before the observance of the Sabbath (a peculiarly Jewish institution) fell into the background and lapsed. The substitution of Sunday for Saturday as the weekly 'holy day' occurred so early in the progress of the Christian mission that no hint is found in the New Testament of any positive command to keep it or any controversy with regard to its observance. It was already an established fact, and was indeed the germ of the Christian Calendar.

This weekly occurrence was closely linked with the regular gathering of the Christian congregation for Scripture-reading, preaching and the 'breaking of bread' (cf. Acts. 20.7ff).

It is difficult for us to realize how tremendous a break with tradition, and indeed with what was held to be divine command, was this change from the observance of the seventh day of the week to the first. Its purpose was to commemorate the Lord's rising from the dead 'on the first day of the week'—a date noted in each of the four Gospels (St. Matthew 28.1; St. Mark 16.2; St. Luke 24.1; St. John 20.1, 19). From the very earliest days, then, this became a distinguishing mark of the Christian community.

The Easter Cycle

Closely connected with this was the *annual* observance of the events of the Passover-tide at which our Lord suffered in Jerusalem, died and was buried, and rose again. Thus began the keeping of Easter, as the liturgical celebration of those central facts of the Christian Gospel and the Christian Church's life. It would seem that this may have been kept at the start as a single feast of Redemption, not till later differentiated into the quasi-historical commemoration of the Cross on Good Friday and the Resurrection on Easter Day. There is no doubt that Easter, generally known as the Passover or the Pasch (cf. 1 Corinthians 5.7, 8) was the 'Feast of Feasts', perhaps the only annual feast. It remained—a historical memorial of the actual events—closely linked with the Passover moon, with which (at any rate till we get a fixed Easter) its date is still connected. This accounts for the vagaries of the actual date of Easter. But there was in the second century a certain variation of practice among Christian communities. Some of those in Asia Minor kept Easter on the actual date of Passover, i.e. of the full moon, on whatever day of the week it should fall. Almost all other Churches insisted that it should always be kept on the first day of the week (that which followed the full moon), and it was this practice which prevailed. Easter was and is, the Sunday of Sundays.

The extension of the Easter feast into a season of rejoicing came early, but we have no record to tell us when. Pentecost, the Jewish Feast of Weeks, or Harvest, fell (as its name implies) on the fiftieth day after Passover, and the gift of the Spirit came to be commemorated on that day. These fifty days were held as one long period of thankfulness for the fact of the Resurrection and the experience of the Resurrection life. Fasting was not allowed, and kneeling for prayer was forbidden. A feast on the fortieth day after Easter as a memorial of the Ascension—Acts 1.3—was a later development.

Thus an 'Easter season' came to be kept. But Easter was not merely an occasion to commemorate a historical fact, the Death and Resurrection of Jesus Christ. St. Paul had emphasized the Christian's personal experience of sharing Christ's Death and Resurrection in the sacrament of baptism (see especially Romans 6.3ff) and by the early third century the celebration of Easter had gained a baptismal character. It became, especially in the Western Church, the principal occasion in the year for the initiation of new converts into the Christian community. This included baptism, the laying on of hands and first admission to communion, and took place in the night leading into Easter Day. It was preceded by a long period of instruction for the candidates. To this, we owe the beginnings of the pre-Easter period which became known as Lent. The closing weeks were of special intensity, marked by successive ceremonies, and the whole congregation came to associate themselves with the final preparation of those who were to join their fellowship by baptism at Easter. The length of this period varied in different parts of the Church. Eventually in the West it settled into a fixed six weeks, of which fasting with prayer and instruction was a dominant feature. As the baptismal connexion fell more into the background, and that of devotional fasting became more prominent, the six weeks tended to become forty weekdays of fasting (Sunday not being a fast day), and thus the beginning of the Fast was pushed back to the Wednesday preceding the sixth Sunday before Easter. This became known as Ash Wednesday, from the penitential ceremony of the blessing and imposition of ashes on the heads of the faithful, and the forty days came to be associated with our Lord's forty days of fasting and temptation in the wilderness.

To return to the days immediately preceding Easter: a shorter or longer fast, often of forty hours, appears as a very early custom, a fast recalling 'the taking away of the bridegroom' (see St. Mark 2.20). But the special commemorations of the week before Easter came into popularity from another source. By the fourth century, Jerusalem had become a noted Christian centre. As was natural in the home-city of the Faith, local observances were held of various events in our Lord's life at the actual spots where they had occurred. We have a detailed description by a Spanish lady named Etheria who visited the Holy City as a pilgrim about A.D. 385. She tells of the procession of palms and olives from Bethany into Jerusalem on the Sunday before Easter (Palm Sunday), of the eucharist on the evening of the Thursday, the gatherings that night on the Mount of Olives, the three hours of our Lord's hanging on the Cross spent at the site of Calvary on the Friday. Thus began the keeping of Holy Week in a kind of historical way, following through the events as they occurred. This was gradually copied in other parts of Christendom, and the more picturesque ceremonies became specially popular in Northern Europe. The habits of Rome itself were more sober and restrained. So the differentiation of the events of the last week of our Lord's life came to be connected with distinct days having their own observances—Palm Sunday, Maundy Thursday (so named from the Mandatum, the command to love one another, emphasized by the feet-washing, a ceremony which still survives), Good Friday the day of the Lord's death, and Easter Even commemorating his burial. The week became known as the Great Week, or Holy Week.

A still further lengthening of the preparation for Easter came at a later period, stretching back the season to the ninth Sunday before Easter. This was, and still is, known as Septuagesima, and the two following Sundays as Sexagesima and Quinquagesima—respectively in Latin the seventieth, sixtieth and fiftieth days before Easter. Quinquagesima is accurate, being literally the fiftieth day before: the others are approximate. But this additional period has never had any very clear purpose—it is a preparation for a preparation—and might well be dispensed with.

So the cycle centred on Easter took shape, stretching from Septuagesima, nine weeks before, till Pentecost or Whitsuntide, fifty days after, a movable block of sixteen weeks.

The Christmas Cycle

We must turn now to the other period, centred on Christmas, which came to be developed on somewhat similar lines. But it differs from the Easter cycle in two ways. First, Easter and its crucial Gospel-events were historically attached to a particular season, whereas the actual date of our Lord's birth was not recorded. Then when an arbitrary date had been decided, it was on a *fixed* date as opposed to the varying dates of the Easter Sunday.

Christian interest in the details of our Lord's birth came much later than in the fundamental facts of his death and resurrection. The Gospels themselves show this: only St. Matthew and St. Luke give a few scattered, and not easily reconcilable, traditions of our Lord's life before the outset of his ministry. But as the great theological controversies on the Person of Christ developed in the early centuries, Christians desired to observe the festival of his incarnation and his birth at Bethlehem liturgically. In fact, two customs appeared. In the East, the date of 6 January was chosen; in the West, that of 25 December. The Easterns knew their feast on 6 January as the Epiphany (Showing, or Manifestation) of Christ. This included his birth, his baptism—which became the dominant theme—and the first sign at Cana at the beginning of his public ministry. At Rome, the chosen date was 25 December, to take the place, perhaps, of the pagan feast of the returning Light at the Winter solstice. Eventually East and West accepted each other's festivals in addition to their own. In the West, 25 December became the commemoration of the birth of Christ, while 6 January emphasized the coming of the Magi, with the baptism of Christ and the sign at Cana as minor themes. In the West, however, the baptism of Christ has never received adequate liturgical observance. The two festivals within twelve days of each other have always been uneasily associated, and have occasioned awkwardness in the arrangements of the Calendar. Further, the three days following Christmas have from very early days been assigned in the West to St. Stephen, St. John the Evangelist, and the Innocents (the two former unrelated to the Christmas feast) and succeeded on 1 January, the octave day, by the feast of the Circumcision, leaving a ragged gap before the second Incarnation–feast on 6 January.

From that date lies a period of irregular length, the Sundays and weeks 'after Epiphany', extending forward until the ninth Sunday before Easter. As Easter now stands, this may vary from as many as six Sundays to as few as one, according to the Paschal moon. If Easter is given a fixed date, the lay-out of this period will be greatly simplified.

We must now look at the weeks *before* Christmas. Easter had its season of preparation in Lent, and it came to be thought fitting that this other focus of the Christian Year should have a similar period of preparation. But while Lent had a historical connexion with the baptismal ceremonies of Easter, nothing of the sort can be claimed for Advent. Its length varied greatly, and still varies. In the East, a fast goes back to mid-November. At Milan, five weeks are still kept. At Rome, and in most parts of the Western Church, the fourth Sunday before Christmas came to be settled as Advent Sunday, and this was regarded as the first day of the Christian Year. Other days have at different times been so regarded in the West—Easter, Christmas, Septuagesima among them—while the Orthodox Church regards the beginning of the Church's Year as occurring in September. We should perhaps be more realistic in seeing the Christian Year as a circle rather than as a straight line. In regard to Advent, for instance, the traditional Scripture lessons (epistles and gospels) for some weeks preceding Advent Sunday already take on an 'Advent' note, and a series of 'Stir up' collects in the Latin service begins on the Sunday before Advent. This 'Advent' note is more specifically the message of the Coming of Christ in glory and the Last Judgement. But this is not maintained consistently, and other themes appear, particularly those of the Old Testament preparation for Christ, and the immediate preparation for his coming into the world at Bethlehem. It is therefore a mistake to regard Advent as a strict parallel with Lent. Advent looks back from the coming of the historic Christ into the world, and forward to his ultimate Triumph. It is a time of solemnity, but also of joyful expectation, as well as one of preparation for the keeping of Christmas.

This Advent–Christmas–Epiphany cycle forms another block of the developed Christian Year. If we think chronologically in terms of the Christian Year as commemorating our Lord's earthly life, it comes earlier than the Easter cycle. But as we have seen, its origins were later, and different in character. Between the two blocks there is a gap, and about half the year remains after Pentecost unallocated to any special season or commemoration. In the larger part of Christendom, these Sundays are denoted as Sundays 'after Pentecost'. In the West during the Middle Ages the first

Sunday after Pentecost came to be observed as a festival in honour of the Holy Trinity, a commemoration not of an event so much as of a doctrine. This was specially popular in Northern Europe, where the Sundays following it until Advent took its name, and were known as Sundays after Trinity. Anglican and Lutheran Christians retain this custom, as do some of the Roman monastic orders, though the Roman Catholic Church as a whole speaks of them as Sundays after Pentecost. Recent revisions of the Calendar, for example in the Church of South India and in service books of the Presbyterian Churches of Ireland and Canada, have restored the earlier and more significant title. We recommend its adoption. With the gift of the Spirit at Pentecost the Church went out into the world to live the Spirit-filled life, and we propose that the Scripture passages assigned to the season should be 'controlled' by lections from the Acts and the Epistles, which record or describe this experience.

What of the Future?

This brief historical introduction has sought to give some account of how the Western Church has gained its present Calendar of Time. The Calendar of Saints (*Sanctorale*) is tied to fixed dates of commemoration, and the two sometimes clash awkwardly and give rise to complicated rules of precedence, laying down which is the more important feast to observe. It is to be hoped that a revision of the *Sanctorale* (Saints' Days which shall, or may, be observed) will be undertaken. But this leads on from the history of the past to suggestions for the future.

The growth of the Christian Year has, as we have seen, been haphazard, a long process, by no means uniform all over the Church, influenced and sometimes distorted by varied interests—theological, historical, liturgical and even topographical. Many of these are no longer relevant, and only serve to complicate the main lines of the picture. We cannot indeed start afresh and disregard history and centuries of devotion. But we may be able to remove some of the features which blur the general effect, and do some tidying-up and (maybe) improvement. A modest attempt at this is offered at the end of this book. It needs some justification and explanation both of the principles on which it has been made, and possibly of detail.

The Christian Year, as it has developed, has come to cover, in the earlier half of each year, the outlines of the life of Christ from his Incarnation to his Ascension and the gift of the Spirit. This is intended, as we have seen, both to elicit thankful remembrance of his mighty acts, and to renew their power in the life of the Christian and the Church. The three foci of the Christian Year are thus Christmas, Easter and Pentecost or Whitsunday. The two former are provided with a period 'before' and 'after'. Pentecost is at once a climax, and a fresh starting point. But there are some minor problems which would be the better for adjustment and simplification.

(1) It is a frequent cause of surprise that immediately after Christmas Day, which has been well prepared for, the attention of worshippers is switched at once to the first martyr, Saint Stephen; there follow St. John the Evangelist, and the massacre of the Innocents (though this of course occurs among the traditions of our Lord's childhood). It would be advisable to allow the Christmas theme to be carried on, and the Feast of the Circumcision on 1 January might well lapse. Nothing would prevent those who wished to observe these commemorations from doing so when they

fell on weekdays, or if one of them happened to be the Patronal Festival of their parish church.

(2) The next crux is the proximity of Christmas Day and Epiphany, and the consequent 'change of step' after 6 January. Our proposal is that the Sundays should run through 'after Christmas' without break, until the Christmas cycle meets the beginning of the Easter cycle. January 6th has come in the Western Church to be regarded principally as the commemoration of the visit of the Magi, and this, at present usually occurring on a weekday, would be kept on a Sunday. The Baptism of Christ should also be given specific commemoration on a Sunday. It is regarded in the Gospels as a highly significant occasion in the life of our Lord, and has never—in the West at least—received the liturgical recognition due to its theological importance. Rome has plans to provide this. The Church of South India has done so. This would be an enrichment of our understanding of our Lord, and the link between his Baptism and ours.

(3) The 'Sundays after Epiphany' have hitherto had the character of filling in a vacant and indefinite period. A fixed Easter would greatly help by reducing this to a regular number of Sundays between Christmas Day and the ninth Sunday before Easter. This would make possible a continuous course of Gospel-reading Sunday by Sunday, bringing to our attention significant events or typical teachings and miracles in the life of Christ in an orderly sequence. (Though this essay deals with the Calendar, the lessons proposed cannot be kept out of the discussion.)

(4) We thus come to the beginning of the Easter cycle. A good case could be made for this to start with the first Sunday in Lent, or with Ash Wednesday four days earlier. The weeks of Septuagesima, Sexagesima, and Quinquagesima

are anomalous. They have no clear function in the orderly progress of the Christian Year. Their names are not easily understood. Traditionally their themes have been taken to be Creation, the Fall of Man, and the call of Abraham, the father of the chosen People, God's vehicle of redemption. These have been taken, abnormally, not from the lessons at the Eucharist but from the Breviary, which begins the reading of Genesis on Septuagesima Sunday; (this has been followed in successive Sunday Lectionaries for Morning and Evening Prayer in the Church of England). These Genesis themes are important, and should find a place somewhere in the year, but it is not obvious that this is the most appropriate occasion. We suggest that the series of Gospels should continue from the Christmas cycle with significant events in the life of Christ leading through uninterruptedly to the Passion, Death and Resurrection. The Temptation in the Wilderness is so closely connected with the opening of Lent that it is best retained on the Sunday after Ash Wednesday. A further advantage of such a scheme would be that not only the Baptism of Christ, but certain other events in our Lord's life which are now observed only on weekdays would find a place on Sundays. These include the Epiphany, the Presentation in the Temple, his recognition by Peter as Messiah, and the Transfiguration. This has hitherto been a minor festival on 6 August; but it clearly belongs to the period preceding the Passion, and should have Sunday rank.

(5) To turn back now to the pre-Christmas period. As we have noted, the themes of Advent have not been clearly distinguished, and the compilers of the English Prayer books have made this confusion worse confounded by emphasizing on the second and third Sundays the Bible and the Ministry respectively. These are not specially 'Advent' subjects, and could well appear elsewhere. There would thus seem to be

a good case for rationalization. The need to rehabilitate the Old Testament as the background of the Christian Gospel is often expressed, and this season of preparation for commemorating Christ's incarnation would appear to give the opportunity. Four Sundays do not give enough scope, especially if the traditional figure of John the Forerunner comes into the scene towards Christmas. We suggest also that this is the right place for the Annunciation of the Blessed Virgin, at present observed on 25 March usually in the middle of Lent. We therefore propose a longer pre-Christmas period. This might stretch back into the later part of the Pentecost season or appear before Advent Sunday, and provide nine Sundays (comparable to the nine Sundays before Easter) concentrating on the preparation in the Old Testament for Christ. Thus the Creation and the Fall would have proper recognition (if removed from Septuagesima), and come in their most convenient place.

Such alterations as these would make for a Calendar more clear in its outline and more helpful to the Sunday worshipper without jettisoning the main scheme of the Christian Year as it has come down to us.

THE LECTIONARY

N. CLARK

THE Lectionary system belongs to the tradition of the Church and is a facet of her ongoing life. It has been tested, revised and proved over many centuries. To lay hands upon it is to touch near the beating heart of her corporate worship. The probe must therefore be delicate and sensitive. The Lectionary cannot be treated with academic detachment or re-created *in toto* as a contemporary exercise in scholarly ingenuity. Though the Church lives in today, her roots are in yesterday.

Yet there are compelling reasons for the conclusion that a marginal revision cannot be accepted as the adequate solution for our time. We are heirs to a revolution in attitude to and understanding of Holy Scripture. This does not mean that the Lectionary must be remodelled in accordance with debatable or transitory 'critical' presuppositions. It does mean that significant insights in regard to Scripture must be allowed to find proper expression in lectionary terms.

To this must be added a full recognition of the mass of new knowledge which liturgical scholarship has made available. In recent generations the past has been so illumined, that our picture of it has necessarily been transformed. Though much still remains dark, we begin to discern the outlines of lectionary growth. We see how much was unplanned, how much was the result of historical accident, how much was due to local pressures and preoccupations. We understand more clearly that the lectionaries to which we are accustomed reflect the age-old divisions of Christendom and represent variants of a tradition which itself is basically western. This does not mean a wholesale rejection of the tangled past, on the superficial assumption that the Holy Spirit is absent from the vicissitudes of history. It does mean that the new light must be allowed to do its searching work, that the new knowledge must be allowed to inform judgement, that the quest for the balance and wholeness of tradition must be allowed to find expression in the Lectionary.

In the light of this general understanding, certain principles of lectionary construction may be found to emerge:

(1) Lectionary tradition must stand under theological control. Clearly the liturgical Lectionary should not be created *de novo*, and heavy weight must be accorded to the inherited wisdom of the centuries. But radical revision is not to be ruled out *a priori*. The 'great liturgical tradition of the West' is not self-justifying. It must be brought to the bar of Scripture, theology, and the wholeness of Tradition.

(2) The primary concern is with the Lectionary that belongs to the (eucharistic) Liturgy. This issue is complicated by inherited practices. Some church traditions have three Services—Mattins, Eucharist, Evensong. Other church traditions have two Services—Morning Worship and Evening Worship, with Holy Communion periodically connected with one or the other or both. The provision of more than one Lectionary has accordingly been inevitable.

Though the need for such provision remains, a clear distinction in thought must here be made. The fundamental construction is the liturgical Lectionary, designed for the Service of Word and Sacrament; or for a Service which, though the Sacrament is not celebrated, follows the same order.

(3) The liturgical Lectionary should be unvarying, but should cover a two-yearly period. Since the Lectionary belongs essentially within the framework of the Calendar, a strong case can be made for the conclusion that it should cover the period of one year only. Present experience, however, confirms the experience of the past in dictating the necessity of a double Lectionary, if anything like adequate presentation of the rich sweep of Scripture is to be obtained.

(4) Old Testament and New Testament lections form the basic and indispensable requirement. Where the reading of the Old Testament is absent from the Liturgy, its reintroduction is an urgent need. It is the assumption of the necessity for the provision of both Epistle and Gospel that may need justification.

Equal weight should be given to two realities. One is that the whole of the New Testament—Gospels and Epistles alike—is 'new covenant' or 'gospel'. The other is that the books bearing special witness to the incarnate life of our Lord must be given a distinctive recognition proper in the light of the events which they record. The result confirms the wisdom of the practice of the three lections—Old Testament, Epistle, and Gospel. These the Lectionary must provide. Yet it also suggests that, if a proper balance is to be preserved, the Gospel should not always be the controlling lection. To say this is to echo the conclusion reached by way of an examination of the Calendar.

(5) The Christian Year began initially at Easter; then Christmas became its beginning; finally its beginning was moved to Advent. But what is left unprovided for is an adequate introduction to the coming of the Christ. If the heart of the Christian Year is Christmas to Pentecost, this period should be preceded by a preparation, strong in its own right and beginning at Creation. Furthermore, it should

be followed by an outworking, strong in its own right and concerned with the life and mission of the People of God who live between Pentecost and Parousia and are on pilgrimage to the ends of the earth and the end of time. To view this progression from the scriptural perspective is surely to reach clear lectionary conclusions. In the pre-Christmas period, the Old Testament should provide the controlling lection. In the post-Pentecost period, the Acts and Epistles should provide the controlling lection. From Christmas to Pentecost, the Gospel should control.

The detailed working out of these principles will become apparent in the discussion of the Lectionary passages. It is necessary, however, to preface that discussion by drawing attention to some significant conclusions which govern compilation.

The primary aim is to let Scripture speak and impose its own terms. It is to give place to the totality of biblical revelation in all the diversity of its witness. The structure of a Calendar which is, in the broadest sense, a faithful reflection of Scripture, rightly and inevitably has a certain determining influence. Yet it must be recognized that this influence is most specific in the pre-Pentecost period, and that for obvious reasons the guide lines are less clear once Pentecost is passed. It is tempting to adopt a thematic approach for the post-Pentecost season; but this is to be rejected both as being a departure from principles governing the treatment of the rest of the Christian year and as being particularly exposed to an arbitrary subjectivism. Rather must the Bible be allowed to dictate its own conclusions.

Concretely, this involves a search of the Epistles, a careful listening to them, a careful selection from them. It may be objected that this also is a subjective procedure; and this indeed cannot be denied. Yet there are certain subsidiary checks that may and must be brought into operation. In the first place, particular attention must be given to traditional lections. This remains true even when it is remembered that the traditional solution was really to move through the Epistles more or less in course, and that this *procedure* is rejected as contrary to the basic principles we have enunciated. For the passages selected and used by the Church through the ages have an obvious inherent claim, even if the ordering of them must be questioned. In this way, due weight is given to the mind of the Church as it was formed over the centuries, while slavish traditionalism is avoided.

But there is a second check that is allowed to operate. For proper weight is given to a sort of *regula fidei*. This means that recognition is given to the fact that all Scripture is not of equal significance, that there are certain passages of special significance, and that in order to represent the wholeness of witness a balance in selection must be observed. All this leaves us still with the problem and the dangers of subjectivity. How could it be otherwise? What may be argued is that this approach is more true to Scripture and more satisfactory in principle than a procedure which would operate by first choosing themes and then selecting biblical passages to exemplify them.

It will be noticed that each Sunday in the Christian Year is in fact provided with its theme. What this practice actually means and how the details were arrived at must be made clear, if misunderstanding is to be avoided. In the pre-Pentecost period, where the Christian Year is most closely and specifically structured, the calendrical control has obviously been heavily determinative. In the post-Pentecost period, the biblical passages were *first* selected, bearing in mind the general thrust of the season, and only then were they ordered and given sequence so that some general progression of theme emerged. It cannot be too strongly emphasized that the thematic titles provided are no more than *indications* of emphasis. They must not be allowed to give false rigidity to the hearing of Scripture or the preaching of the Word of God. The lections are, on the whole, rich in material. They may say different things to different people, and it is right that they should do so.

Once the *controlling* lections were selected, and the indications of emphasis plotted, the allied readings were chosen. An attempt has been made to ensure that, as far as possible, they 'support' the controlling lection. It has been felt to be specially important, in this connexion, that the proper correspondence between the two Testaments should be presented and made clear. The lectionary for the second year closely echoes that for the first in pattern and method of production. Care has been taken to ensure that the two together constitute a balanced whole and that, within the inescapable limits, those passages of Scripture which *should* be read are in fact included.

9th Sunday before Christmas to Christmas

The Old Testament lection controls throughout. During this season, the movement from creation to incarnation reveals the ongoing divine purpose and promise at focal points in the historical revelation. In the early part, special attention is given to the first half of Genesis. During the traditional 'Advent' preparation nearer to Christmas, the prophetic witness dominates.

9th before Christmas. The Creation
8th before Christmas. The Fall
7th before Christmas. The Covenant of Preservation: Noah

6th before Christmas. The Election of God's People: Abraham

5th before Christmas. The Promise of Redemption: Moses

4th before Christmas. The Advent Hope

3rd before Christmas. The Word of God in the Old Testament

2nd before Christmas. The Forerunner

1st before Christmas. The Annunciation.

Over the centuries, Advent has come to have a double reference—to the Nativity and to the Second Advent. The interconnection is real and significant; and in view of this, the Epistle and Gospel for the 4th Sunday before Christmas (Advent 1) in both years strike the future note.

Christmas to Easter

Christmas 1.	The Wise Men
Christmas 2.	The Presentation in the Temple (1st Year)
	The Visit to Jerusalem (2nd Year)
Christmas 3.	The Baptism of Christ
Christmas 4.	The First Disciples
Christmas 5.	The First Sign:
	The Wedding at Cana (1st Year)
	The New Temple (2nd Year)
Christmas 6.	The Friend of Sinners (1st Year)
	Life for the World (2nd Year)
9th before Easter.	Christ the Teacher
8th before Easter.	Christ the Healer
7th before Easter.	Christ, Worker of Miracles
6th before Easter.	The King and the Kingdom: Temptation
5th before Easter.	The King and the Kingdom: Conflict

4th before Easter. The King and the Kingdom:
                    Suffering
3rd before Easter. The King and the Kingdom:
                    Transfiguration
2nd before Easter. The King and the Kingdom:
                    Victory of the Cross
1st before Easter. The Way of the Cross.

(1) The Lectionary is framed on the basis of a fixed Easter, occurring always between 9 April and 15 April. It has then to be recognized that, while the Lectionary will in general remain constant, Christmas 6 will disappear whenever Easter Day falls on 9 April (unless it is a Leap Year).

(2) The Gospel lection controls throughout. In some sense Christmas 6 marks a watershed, in that up to that point the movement is away from Christmas while after that point the movement is towards Easter. Yet the whole season possesses an overarching unity and progression rooted in the historical life and ministry of the Lord.

(3) In terms of the Gospels, the Baptism and the Temptations belong together. In terms of the Christian Year, the Baptism should be tied closely to the Epiphany festival, while the Temptations are traditionally associated with the beginning of Lent. This tends to mean that any ordered movement through the Ministry begun during the Christmas season is violently interrupted by a sudden movement back to the Temptations at Lent 1 (6th before Easter). While it has not seemed right to disturb such proper or traditional calendrical associations, an attempt has been made to give greater coherence to the whole season.

(4) The lectionary selections for Christmas 4, 5 and 6, hold thought back from too rapid a movement into the Ministry. Attention is first directed to the calling of the

disciples. Then two great notes are struck which, in a real way, characterize or epitomize the Ministry as a whole. From the Johannine witness are taken the great introductory 'signs' which speak of the new order which Christ brings. These are followed, on Christmas 6, by the proclamation of the Lord whether as the Friend of sinners or as Life for the world.

As the movement towards Easter is begun, crucial aspects of the Ministry are summed up by the provision of typical teaching (whether in sermons to the disciples or in parables to the crowds), of typical healing (which, in the first year, is revealed as reaching to the whole man), and of typical miracle. With the beginning of Lent (6th before Easter), the drive becomes more purposeful. Central to the Ministry is the Kingdom of God. This is, in fact, the true context of the Temptations. The traditional Lenten lection is accordingly extended (in the first year) to make this clear; and in both years there is initiated a coherent series that moves through Caesarea Philippi and the Transfiguration to the Cross and Resurrection, and deals with the King and the Kingdom.

Easter to Pentecost

    Easter 1. The Upper Room Appearances (1st Year)
                The Bread of Life (2nd Year)
    Easter 2. The Emmaus Road (1st Year)
                The Good Shepherd (2nd Year)
    Easter 3. The Lakeside (1st Year)
                The Resurrection and the Life (2nd Year)
    Easter 4. The Charge to Peter (1st Year)
                The Way, the Truth, and the Life (2nd Year)
    Easter 5. Going to the Father
    Easter 6. The Ascension of Christ
    Pentecost. The Gift of the Spirit.

The Gospel continues to control in the movement towards the Ascension. It seems right that the season should give full place to the events associated with the Resurrection. This is to be preferred to the ancient practice of moving somewhat too quickly to the anticipation of Pentecost. Accordingly, in the first year, the Gospel lections concentrate heavily on the Resurrection appearances. Yet the victory of Christ corresponds and points to the final victory and redemption, to the consummation, to all that belongs to eschatology. What is and what will be are properly linked at this season. Accordingly, the Epistles treat of these things. In the second year, the appearances are replaced by lections containing 'I am' passages from the Fourth Gospel. As concentrating on the reality of life eternal, and as represented as coming from the lips of the Lord who is already, in some sense, conqueror of death, these passages are specially appropriate here.

Pentecost 1-21

The Epistle lection controls throughout. Here the Church moves forward from the Cross and Resurrection, in the light of the Ascension, and under the gift of the Holy Spirit. The baptized move forward from their baptism. The concern is with the life of the People of God travailing in history 'between the times'.

Pentecost 1, Year 1. The Riches of God
                    2. The Church's Message
Pentecost 2, Year 1. The People of God
                    2. The Church's Unity and Fellowship
Pentecost 3, Year 1. The Life of the Baptized
                    2. The Church's Confidence in Christ
Pentecost 4, Year 1. The Freedom of the Sons of God
                    2. The Church's Mission to the Individual

Pentecost 5, Year 1. The New Law
                  2. The Church's Mission to all men

Years 1 and 2

Pentecost 6.	The New Man
Pentecost 7.	The More Excellent Way
Pentecost 8.	The Fruit of the Spirit
Pentecost 9.	The Whole Armour of God.
Pentecost 10.	The Mind of Christ
Pentecost 11.	The Serving Community
Pentecost 12.	The Witnessing Community
Pentecost 13.	The Suffering Community
Pentecost 14.	The Neighbour
Pentecost 15.	The Family
Pentecost 16.	Those in Authority
Pentecost 17.	The Proof of Faith
Pentecost 18.	The Offering of Life
Pentecost 19.	The Life of Faith
Pentecost 20.	Citizens of Heaven
(Pentecost 21.	Endurance.)

(1) In this season especially, the thematic titles provided must be clearly seen to be no more than indications of emphasis. They are not intended to dictate to the biblical material, and should not be allowed to do so.

(2) The same general progression is followed in both lectionaries, except in the first five Sundays after Pentecost. For this period, in the second year, it is felt right that place should be given to the life and work of the Spirit-filled Church. Five readings from the early chapters of the Acts of the Apostles have been selected as controlling lections. They deal with the Church's message, the apostolic kerygma (Acts 2.22–24, 32–36), the Church's unity and fellowship (Acts 2.37–47), the Church's confidence in Christ as the only

Saviour and Lord (Acts 4.5–12), and the Church's mission to individuals (Acts 8.26–38) and to all men and nations (Acts 11.4–18).

(3) The lectionary progression reaches its real conclusion at Pentecost 20. It is only when 22 October falls on a Sunday that Pentecost 21 becomes necessary. The lections provided may be found to exemplify 'Endurance'.

(4) The progression of thought so far as the controlling lections are concerned may be adjudged self-evident. In the first year lectionary it may be noted that a series of five Old Testament lections from Exodus and Deuteronomy occurs at the beginning of the period. The preoccupation is with the significant features of the immediate post-Exodus experience. Here it is shown that as the Church moves forward from the Cross-Resurrection deliverance on pilgrimage to the eternal city, so Israel moved forward from the Exodus deliverance on pilgrimage to the Promised Land. Somewhat similarly, at Pentecost 11, 12, and 13, the marks of the Church set forth in the Epistles are linked to the mission of God's ancient people by the use of three of the Servant Songs of Isaiah as Old Testament lections.

(5) It seemed right that the Farewell Discourse should be heard by the Church at the post-Pentecost season. A substantial part of John 13–17 has therefore been used in the first year for Gospel lections.

It remains to speak of the Liturgical Lectionary viewed in its entirety. How far is it adequate to its purpose? How nearly does it do justice to the balance of Scripture?

(1) It is important that the total amount of Scripture enjoined for any one Sunday shall not be excessive. The proper balance of the various parts of the Liturgy must be maintained. The demands upon the congregation must not

be unrealistic. Yet it is equally urgent that the reading of Scripture shall be allowed proper and sufficient place. In general, it is felt that thirty verses may be deemed desirable. The *average* lectionary provision is, in fact, 29 verses in the first year and 30 verses in the second. The minimum Sunday provision is 19 verses in the first year and 17 verses in the second. The maximum Sunday provision is 40 verses in the first year and 41 verses in the second. It is strongly to be urged that whenever possible, all three lections should be read. If only two lections are read, one of them should always be the controlling lection for the day in question.

It is recognized that where two lections only are used some extension of the passages may be welcomed. For this reason, some lengthening of the Old Testament lection is, in places, suggested. The provision of an extension to the Good Friday Gospel lection takes into account the special circumstances of the day. The only alternatives provided are an Old Testament lection that may, if desired, replace the passage from the Apocrypha set for Pentecost 18 (2nd Year), and a Palm Sunday Gospel lection that may be more suitable in the special circumstances of Holy Week.

(2) The total number of verses used from the Bible is 3,212. Of these, 991 are taken from the Old Testament, 11 from the Apocrypha, and 2,210 from the New Testament. All books from the Old and New Testaments are represented with the exception of Numbers, Judges, 2 Chronicles, Ezra, Esther, Ecclesiastes, Song of Solomon, Lamentations, Obadiah, Nahum, Habakkuk, Haggai, 2 Thessalonians, 2 John, 3 John, and Jude. The book of Psalms is excluded as being a treasury of prayer and praise. Ecclesiasticus is used from the Apocrypha.

In the Old Testament there is heavy concentration upon Genesis, Exodus, and Isaiah—as is fitting with books of such importance both intrinsically and in terms of background to the New Testament. Yet within the limits of possibility, attempt has been made to give representation to the narratives of Old Testament history. From the major and minor prophets 235 verses are taken in the first year and 196 in the second; and from the rest of the Old Testament 244 verses in the first year and 367 in the second.

In the New Testament (apart from the Gospels) special attention is given to Romans, 1 Corinthians, Ephesians, and Hebrews. From the Gospels 679 verses are taken in the first year and 659 in the second; and from the rest of the New Testament 529 verses are taken in the first year and 554 in the second. The complete Lectionary uses 257 verses of Matthew, 139 of Mark, 393 of Luke, and 401 of John.

(3) Comparison of the first and second year lectionaries will reveal certain duplication of lections. These mainly occur at the special observances of Christmas Day, Good Friday, Easter Day, and Ascension Day. To these must be added Christmas 1 (The Magi) and Easter 6 (Ascension). The only remaining instances are the use of Isaiah 42.1–7 at Pentecost 11 in the first year and Christmas 3 in the second year, and the use of John 1.1–14 in the first year both at 9th before Christmas and on Christmas Day.

The Lectionary assumes the establishment of a fixed Easter, which is presumed to fall between 9 April and 15 April. It should be noted that on the basis of this reckoning Pentecost 21 will be required only when 22 October is a Sunday, and Christmas 6 will disappear whenever Easter Day falls on 9 April (unless it is a Leap Year).

It is strongly hoped that a fixed Easter will be established quickly. Meanwhile, some modifications must be made appropriately in the use of the Lectionary. Additional lections may be used as follows:

Extra Sundays after Christmas

(1) Joel 2.15–22;   2 Corinthians 3.4–11;   Mark 2.18–22
(2) Isaiah 1.10–17; 1 Corinthians 3.18–23; Mark 2.23–3.6

Extra Sundays after Pentecost

(1) Exodus 19.16–24;   Hebrews 12.18–29;   John 4.19–26
(2) Lamentations 3.19–26;   1 Thessalonians 5.12–24;
                                    Matthew 20.1–15

THE CALENDAR AND THEMES

9th Sunday before Christmas
  The Creation
8th Sunday before Christmas
  The Fall
7th Sunday before Christmas
  The Covenant of Preservation: Noah
6th Sunday before Christmas
  The Election of God's People: Abraham
5th Sunday before Christmas
  The Promise of Redemption: Moses
4th Sunday before Christmas (Advent 1)
  The Advent Hope
3rd Sunday before Christmas (Advent 2)
  The Word of God in the Old Testament
2nd Sunday before Christmas (Advent 3)
  The Forerunner
1st Sunday before Christmas (Advent 4)
  The Annunciation
CHRISTMAS DAY
  The Birth of Christ
Christmas 1
  The Wise Men
Christmas 2
  (1st Year)   The Presentation in the Temple
  (2nd Year) The Visit to Jerusalem
Christmas 3
  The Baptism of Christ

Christmas 4
  The First Disciples
Christmas 5
  The First Sign: (1st Year) The Wedding at Cana
                   (2nd Year) The New Temple
Christmas 6
  (1st Year)   The Friend of Sinners
  (2nd Year) Life for the World
9th Sunday before Easter
  Christ the Teacher
8th Sunday before Easter
  Christ the Healer
7th Sunday before Easter
  Christ, Worker of Miracles
6th Sunday before Easter (Lent 1)
  The King and the Kingdom: Temptation
5th Sunday before Easter (Lent 2)
  The King and the Kingdom: Conflict
4th Sunday before Easter (Lent 3)
  The King and the Kingdom: Suffering
3rd Sunday before Easter (Lent 4)
  The King and the Kingdom: Transfiguration
2nd Sunday before Easter (Passion)
  The King and the Kingdom: Victory of the Cross
1st Sunday before Easter (Palm)
  The Way of the Cross
GOOD FRIDAY
  The Death of Christ
EASTER DAY
  The Resurrection of Christ
Easter 1
  (1st Year)   The Upper Room Appearances
  (2nd Year) The Bread of Life

Easter 2
  (1st Year)   The Emmaus Road
  (2nd Year) The Good Shepherd
Easter 3
  (1st Year)   The Lakeside
  (2nd Year) The Resurrection and the Life
Easter 4
  (1st Year)   The Charge to Peter
  (2nd Year) The Way, the Truth and the Life
Easter 5
  Going to the Father
ASCENSION DAY
  The Ascension of Christ
Easter 6 (Ascension Sunday)
  The Ascension of Christ
PENTECOST
  The Gift of the Spirit
Pentecost 1 (Trinity Sunday)
  (1st Year)   The Riches of God
  (2nd Year) The Church's Message
Pentecost 2
  (1st Year)   The People of God
  (2nd Year) The Church's Unity and Fellowship
Pentecost 3
  (1st Year)   The Life of the Baptized
  (2nd Year) The Church's Confidence in Christ
Pentecost 4
  (1st Year)   The Freedom of the Sons of God
  (2nd Year) The Church's Mission to the Individual
Pentecost 5
  (1st Year)   The New Law
  (2nd Year) The Church's Mission to all Men

Pentecost 6
  The New Man
Pentecost 7
  The More Excellent Way
Pentecost 8
  The Fruit of the Spirit
Pentecost 9
  The Whole Armour of God
Pentecost 10
  The Mind of Christ
Pentecost 11
  The Serving Community
Pentecost 12
  The Witnessing Community
Pentecost 13
  The Suffering Community
Pentecost 14
  The Neighbour
Pentecost 15
  The Family
Pentecost 16
  Those in Authority
Pentecost 17
  The Proof of Faith
Pentecost 18
  The Offering of Life
Pentecost 19
  The Life of Faith
Pentecost 20
  Citizens of Heaven
Pentecost 21
  Endurance

NOTE

If there is a desire to regard the Church's Year as still beginning on the first Sunday in Advent, the five pre-Advent Sundays may be placed at the end of the Calendar and designated as Sundays after Pentecost viz.

9th Sunday before Christmas (Pentecost 22)
8th Sunday before Christmas (Pentecost 23)
7th Sunday before Christmas (Pentecost 24)
6th Sunday before Christmas (Pentecost 25)
5th Sunday before Christmas (Sunday next before Advent)

THE LECTIONARY

[Bold type denotes the 'controlling lesson' for each day]

First Year

Sunday	Old Testament
9th before Christmas	**Genesis** 1.1–3, 24–31a
8th before Christmas	**Genesis** 3.1–15
7th before Christmas	**Genesis** 8.13–22
6th before Christmas	**Genesis** 12.1–9
5th before Christmas	**Exodus** 3.1–15
4th before Christmas (Advent 1)	**Isaiah** 52.1–10
3rd before Christmas (Advent 2)	**Isaiah** 55.1–11
2nd before Christmas (Advent 3)	**Isaiah** 40.1–11
1st before Christmas (Advent 4)	**Isaiah** 11.1–9
Christmas Day (i)	Micah 5.2–4
Christmas Day (ii)	Isaiah 9.2–7
Christmas 1	Isaiah 60.1–6
Christmas 2	1 Samuel 1.20–28
Christmas 3	1 Samuel 16.1–13
Christmas 4	Jeremiah 1.4–10
Christmas 5	Exodus 33.12–23
Christmas 6	Hosea 14.1–7
9th before Easter	Isaiah 30.18–21
8th before Easter	Zephaniah 3.14–20
7th before Easter	Deuteronomy 8.1–6
Ash Wednesday	Isaiah 58.1–8
6th before Easter (Lent 1)	Deuteronomy 30.15–20
5th before Easter (Lent 2)	2 Kings 6.8–17
4th before Easter (Lent 3)	Isaiah 59.15–20

Epistle	Gospel
. Colossians 1.15–20	John 1.1–14
. Romans 7.7–12	John 3.13–21
. Romans 3.21–26	Luke 12.1–7
. Romans 4.13–25	John 8.51–58
. Hebrews 3.1–6	John 6.27–35
. 1 Thessalonians 5.1–11	Luke 21.25–33
. Romans 15.4–13	John 5.36–47
. 1 Corinthians 4.1–5	John 1.19–27
. 1 Corinthians 1.26–31	Luke 1.26–38
. Titus 2.11–15	**Luke** 2.1–20
. 1 John 4.7–14	**John** 1.1–14
. Hebrews 1.1–4	**Matthew** 2.1–12
. Romans 12.1–8	**Luke** 2.21–40
. Acts 10.34–48	**Matthew** 3.13–17
. Acts 26.1, 9–18	**Mark** 1.14–20
. 1 John 1.1–4	**John** 2.1–11
. Philemon 1–16	**Mark** 2.13–17
. 1 Corinthians 4.8–13	**Matthew** 5.1–12
. James 5.13–16	**Mark** 2.1–12
. Philippians 4.10–20	**John** 6.1–14
. 1 Corinthians 9.24–27	**Matthew** 6.16–21
. Hebrews 2.14–18	**Matthew** 4.1–17
. 1 John 4.1–6	**Luke** 11.14–26
. 1 Peter 2.19–25	**Matthew** 16.13–28

Sunday	Old Testament
3rd before Easter (Lent 4)	Exodus 34.29–35 . . . . .
2nd before Easter (Passion)	Isaiah 63.1–9 . . . .
1st before Easter (Palm)	Zechariah 9.9–12 . . . . .
Good Friday	Exodus 12.1–11 . . . . . .
Easter Day (i)	Isaiah 12.1–6 . . . .
Easter Day (ii)	Exodus 14.15–22 . . . . . .
Easter 1	Exodus 15.1–11 . . . . . .
Easter 2	Isaiah 25.6–9 . . . .
Easter 3	Isaiah 61.1–3 . . . .
Easter 4	Isaiah 62.1–5 . . . .
Easter 5	Isaiah 51.1–6 . . . .
Ascension Day	Daniel 7.13–14 . . . . . .
Easter 6	Daniel 7.9–14 . . . . . .
Pentecost	Joel 2.23–29 . . . .
Pentecost 1 (Trinity)	Isaiah 6.1–8 . . . .
Pentecost 2	Exodus 19.1–6 . . . . . .
Pentecost 3	Deuteronomy 6.17–25 . . .
Pentecost 4	Deuteronomy 7.6–9a . . . .
Pentecost 5	Exodus 20.1–17 . . . . . .
Pentecost 6	Exodus 24.3–8 . . . . . .
Pentecost 7	Hosea 11.1–9 . . . .
Pentecost 8	Ezekiel 36.24–28 . . . . . .
Pentecost 9	Joshua 1.1–9 . . . .
Pentecost 10	Job 42.1–6 . . . .
Pentecost 11	Isaiah 42.1–7 . . . .
Pentecost 12	Isaiah 49.1–6 . . . .
Pentecost 13	Isaiah 50.4–9 . . . .
Pentecost 14	Leviticus 19.9–18 . . . .
Pentecost 15	Isaiah 54.1–8 . . . .
Pentecost 16	Isaiah 45.1–7 . . . .
Pentecost 17	Jeremiah 7.1–7 . . . . . .
Pentecost 18	Deuteronomy 26.1–11 . . .

Epistle	*Gospel*
. . 2 Corinthians 3.12–18	**Matthew** 17.1–8
. . Colossians 2.8–15	**John** 12.20–32
. . 1 Corinthians 1.18–25	**Mark** 11.1–11 (or **Matthew** 26, 27.1–61)
. . Hebrews 10.11–25.	**John** (18 &) 19.1–37
. . Revelation 1.12–18	**Mark** 16.1–8
. . 1 Corinthians 15.12–20	**John** 20.1–18
. . 1 Peter 1.3–9	**John** 20.19–29
. . Revelation 19.6–9	**Luke** 24.13–35
. . 1 Corinthians 15.1–11	**John** 21.1–14
. . Revelation 3.14–22	**John** 21.15–22
. . 1 Corinthians 15.21–28	**John** 16.25–33
. . Acts 1.1–11	**Matthew** 28.16–20
. . Ephesians 1.15–23	**Luke** 24.44–53
. . **Acts** 2.1–11	John 14.15–27
. . **Ephesians** 1.3–14	John 14.8–17
. . **1 Peter** 2.1–10	John 15.1–5
. . **Romans** 6.1–11	John 15.6–11
. . **Galatians** 3.26 – 4.7	John 15.12–15
. . **Ephesians** 5.1–10	Matthew 19.16–26
. . **Colossians** 3.12–17	Luke 15.11–32
. . 1 **Corinthians** 13.1–13	Matthew 18.21–35
. . **Galatians** 5.16–25	John 15.16–27
. . **Ephesians** 6.10–18a	John 17.11–19
. . **Philippians** 2.1–13	John 13.1–15
. . 2 **Corinthians** 4.1–10	John 13.33–36
. . 2 **Corinthians** 5.14–21	John 17.20–26
. . 1 **Peter** 4.12–19	John 16.1–11
. . **Romans** 12.9–21	Luke 10.25–37
. . **Ephesians** 5.21 – 6.4	Mark 10.2–16
. . **Romans** 13.1–7	Matthew 22.15–22
. . **James** 1.22–27	Matthew 7.21–29
. . 2 **Corinthians** 8.1–9	Matthew 5.21–26

Sunday	*Old Testament*
Pentecost 19	Genesis 28.10–22 . . . . . .
Pentecost 20	Jeremiah 29.1, 4–14. . . . .
Pentecost 21	Daniel 3.13–25. . . . . . .

1. If Epiphany is celebrated on 6 January, the lessons will be
Isaiah 60.1–6. . . . .

2. Matthew 26, 27.1–61 is inserted as an alternative on Palm Sunday on the

Epistle	*Gospel*
. . **Hebrews** 11.1–3, 7–16	Luke 5.1–11
. . **Philippians** 3.7–21	John 17.1–10
. . **Hebrews** 11.32 – 12.2	Luke 9.51–62

. . Revelation 21.22–22.5 . . . . Matthew 2.1–20
or Ephesians 3.1–12

assumption that the Passion narratives may be read throughout Holy Week.

Second Year

Sunday	*Old Testament*
9th before Christmas	**Genesis** 2.4b–9, 15–25 . . .
8th before Christmas	**Genesis** 4.1–10 . . . . . .
7th before Christmas	**Genesis** 9.9–17 . . . . . .
6th before Christmas	**Genesis** 22.1–18 . . . . . .
5th before Christmas	**Exodus** 6.2–8 . . . .
4th before Christmas (Advent 1)	**Isaiah** 51.4–11 . . . . . .
3rd before Christmas (Advent 2)	**Isaiah** 64.1–5 . . . . . .
2nd before Christmas (Advent 3)	**Malachi** 3.1–5 . . . . . .
1st before Christmas (Advent 4)	**Zechariah** 2.10–13 . . . .
Christmas Day (i)	Micah 5.2–4 . . . .
Christmas Day (ii)	Isaiah 9.2–7 . . . .
Christmas 1	Isaiah 49.7–13 . . . . . .
Christmas 2	Deuteronomy 16.1–6 . . . .
Christmas 3	Isaiah 42.1–7 . . . . . .
Christmas 4	1 Samuel 3.1–10 . . . . . .
Christmas 5	1 Kings 8.22–30 . . . . . .
Christmas 6	1 Kings 10.1–13 . . . . . .
9th before Easter	Proverbs 3.1–8 . . . . . .
8th before Easter	2 Kings 5.1–14 . . . . . .
7th before Easter	Jonah 1.1–17 . . . . . .
Ash Wednesday	Amos 5.6–15 . . . .
6th before Easter (Lent 1)	Deuteronomy 6.10–17 . . .
5th before Easter (Lent 2)	Isaiah 35.1–10 . . . . . .
4th before Easter (Lent 3)	Isaiah 45.18–25 . . . . . .
3rd before Easter (Lent 4)	1 Kings 19.1–12 . . . . . .

Epistle	*Gospel*
. Revelation 4.1–11	John 3.1–8
. 1 John 3.9–18	Mark 7.14–23
. Romans 8.18–25	Luke 12.22–31
. James 2.14–24	Luke 20.9–16
. Hebrews 11.17–29.	Mark 13.5–13
. Romans 13.8–14	Matthew 25.31–46
. 2 Timothy 3.14 – 4.5	Luke 4.14–21
. Philippians 4.4–9	Matthew 11.2–15
. Revelation 21.1–7.	Matthew 1.18–23
. Titus 2.11–15	**Luke** 2.1–20
. 1 John 4.7–14.	**John** 1.1–14
. Ephesians 3.1–6	**Matthew** 2.1–12
. Romans 8.12–17	**Luke** 2.41–52
. Ephesians 2.1–10	**John** 1.29–34
. Galatians 1.11–24	**John** 1.35–51
. 1 Corinthians 3.10–17	**John** 2.13–22
. Ephesians 3.8–19	**John** 4.7–14
. 1 Corinthians 2.1–10	**Luke** 8.4–15
. 2 Corinthians 12.1–10	**Mark** 1.35–45
. James 1.2–12	**Mark** 4.35–41
. James 4.1–8a	**Luke** 18.9–14
. Hebrews 4.12–16	**Luke** 4.1–13
. 1 John 3.1–8	**Matthew** 12.22–32
. Colossians 1.24–29	**Luke** 9.18–27
. 2 Peter 1.16–19	**Luke** 9.28–36

Sunday	*Old Testament*
2nd before Easter (Passion)	Jeremiah 31.31–34 . . . . .
1st before Easter (Palm)	Isaiah 52.13 – 53.12 . . . . .
Good Friday	Exodus 12.1–11 . . . . . .
Easter Day (i)	Isaiah 12.1–6 . . . .
Easter Day (ii)	Exodus 14.15–22 . . . . . .
Easter 1	Exodus 16.4–15 . . . . . .
Easter 2	Ezekiel 34.7–15 . . . . . .
Easter 3	1 Kings 17.17–24 . . . . . .
Easter 4	Proverbs 4.10–18 . . . . . .
Easter 5	Deuteronomy 34.1–12 . . . .
Ascension Day	Daniel 7.13–14 . . . .
Easter 6	2 Kings 2.1–15 . . . .
Pentecost	Joel 2.28–32 . . . .
Pentecost 1 (Trinity)	Deuteronomy 6.4–9 . . . . .
Pentecost 2	2 Samuel 7.4–16 . . . . . .
Pentecost 3	Deuteronomy 8.11–20 . . . .
Pentecost 4	Joshua 24.14–25 . . . . . .
Pentecost 5	Ruth 1.8–17, 22 . . . . . .
Pentecost 6	Micah 6.1–8 . . . .
Pentecost 7	Deuteronomy 10.12 – 11.1 . .
Pentecost 8	Ezekiel 37.1–14 . . . . . .
Pentecost 9	1 Samuel 17.37–50 . . . . .
Pentecost 10	1 Samuel 24.9–17 . . . . . .
Pentecost 11	1 Chronicles 29.1–9 . . . . .
Pentecost 12	Micah 4.1–7 . . . .
Pentecost 13	Jeremiah 12.1–6 . . . . . .
Pentecost 14	Deuteronomy 15.7–11 . . . .
Pentecost 15	Genesis 45.1–15 . . . . . .
Pentecost 16	1 Kings 3.5–15 . . . .
Pentecost 17	Jeremiah 32.6–15 . . . . . .
Pentecost 18	Ecclesiasticus 38.24–34 . . . . or Nehemiah 6.1–16 . . . . .
Pentecost 19	Daniel 6.10–23 . . . .

Epistle	*Gospel*
. Hebrews 9.11–15	**Mark** 10.32–45
. Hebrews 10.1–10	**Matthew** 21.1–11
	(or **Matthew** 2 6,27.1–61)
. Hebrews 10.11–25.	**John** (18 &) 19.1–37
. 1 Corinthians 5.7b–8	**Matthew** 28.1–10
. 1 Corinthians 15.12–20	**John** 20.1–18
. 1 Corinthians 15.53–58	**John** 6.35–40
. 1 Peter 5.1–11	**John** 10.7–18
. Colossians 3.1–11	**John** 11.17–27
. 2 Corinthians 4.11–18	**John** 14.1–11
. Romans 8.28–39	**John** 16.12–24
. Acts 1.1–11	**Matthew** 28.16–20
. Ephesians 4.1–8, 11–13	**Luke** 24.44–53
. **Acts** 2.1–11	John 14.15–27
. **Acts** 2.22–24, 32–36	Matthew 11.25–30
. **Acts** 2.37–47.	Luke 14.15–24
. **Acts** 4.5–12	Luke 8.41–55
. **Acts** 8.26–38	Luke 15.1–10
. **Acts** 11.4–18.	Luke 17.11–19
. **Ephesians** 4.17–32	Mark 10.46–52
. **Romans** 8.1–11	Mark 12.28–34
. 1 **Corinthians** 12.4–13	Luke 6.27–38
. 2 **Corinthians** 6.1–10	Mark 9.14–29
. **Galatians** 6.1–10	Luke 7.36–50.
. **Philippians** 1.1–11	Luke 17.5–10
. **Acts** 17.22–31	Matthew 5.13–16
. **Acts** 20.17–35	Matthew 10.16–22
. 1 **John** 4.15–21	Luke 16.19–31
. 1 **Peter** 3.1–9	Luke 14.25–33
. 1 **Timothy** 2.1–7	Luke 11.1–13
. **Galatians** 2.20 – 3.9	Luke 7.1–10
. 1 **Peter** 4.7–11	Matthew 25.14–29
. **Romans** 5.1–11	Luke 19.1–10

Sunday	*Old Testament*
Pentecost 20	Isaiah 33.17–22 . . . .
Pentecost 21	Genesis 32.24–30 . . . . . .

1. If Epiphany is celebrated on 6 January, the lessons will be
                                    Isaiah 60.1–6 . . . .

2. Matthew 26, 27.1–61 is inserted as an alternative on Palm Sunday on the

	Epistle		*Gospel*
.	**Revelation** 7.9–17	. . . .	Matthew 25.1–13
.	1 **Corinthians** 9.19–27	. . . .	Matthew 24.34–46

Revelation 21.22–22.5	. . . .	Matthew 2.1–20
or Ephesians 3.1–12		

ssumption that the Passion narratives may be read throughout Holy Week.

POSSIBLE EXTENSION OF OLD TESTAMENT PASSAGES

(for possible use at services when only two lections are used)

	1st Year	*2nd Year*
9th before Christmas	Genesis 1.1 – 2.3	*stet*
8th before Christmas	Genesis 3.1–24	Genesis 4.1–16
7th before Christmas	Genesis 8.1–22	Genesis 9.1–17
6th before Christmas	*stet*	*stet*
5th before Christmas	Exodus 3.1–22	Exodus 6.2–13
4th before Christmas	*stet*	*stet*
3rd before Christmas	Isaiah 55.1–13	Isaiah 64.1–12
2nd before Christmas	*stet*	Malachi 3.1–5, 4.1–6
1st before Christmas	*stet*	*stet*
Christmas Day (i)	*stet*	*stet*
Christmas Day (ii)	*stet*	*stet*
Christmas 1	Isaiah 60.1–22	Isaiah 49.1–13
Christmas 2	1 Samuel 1.1–28	*stet*
Christmas 3	*stet*	Isaiah 42.1–12
Christmas 4	Jeremiah 1.4–19	1 Samuel 3.1–20
Christmas 5	Exodus 33.7–23	*stet*
Christmas 6	*stet*	*stet*
9th before Easter	Isaiah 30.8–21	Proverbs 3.1–18
8th before Easter	*stet*	2 Kings 5.1–27
7th before Easter	Deuteronomy 8.1–10	*stet*
Ash Wednesday	Isaiah 58.1–12	Amos 5.4–15
6th before Easter	Deuteronomy 30.11–20	*stet*
5th before Easter	2 Kings 6.8–23	*stet*
4th before Easter	Isaiah 59.1–21	Isaiah 45.14–25
3rd before Easter	*stet*	1 Kings 19.1–18
2nd before Easter	Isaiah 63.1–16	*stet*
1st before Easter	*stet*	*stet*
Good Friday	Exodus 12.1–13	Exodus 12.1–13
Easter Day (i)	*stet*	*stet*
Easter Day (ii)	Exodus 14.5–30a	Exodus 14.5–30a

	1st Year	2nd Year
Easter 1	Exodus 15.1–18	Exodus 16.1–15, 31–35
Easter 2	Isaiah 25.1–9	Ezekiel 34.1–15
Easter 3	Isaiah 61.1–11	1 Kings 17.8–24
Easter 4	Isaiah 62.1–12	Proverbs 4.1–18
Easter 5	Isaiah 51.1–16	stet
Ascension Day	stet	stet
Easter 6	stet	stet
Pentecost	Joel 2.21–32	Joel 2.21–32
Pentecost 1	stet	stet
Pentecost 2	Exodus 19.1–11	2 Samuel 7.1–17
Pentecost 3	stet	stet
Pentecost 4	Deuteronomy 7.1–11	Joshua 24.1–5, 14–28
Pentecost 5	stet	Ruth 1.1–22
Pentecost 6	Exodus 24.1–18	stet
Pentecost 7	stet	stet
Pentecost 8	Ezekiel 36.22–32	stet
Pentecost 9	stet	1 Samuel 17.1–11, 32–50
Pentecost 10	Job 38.1–11 & 42.1–6	1 Samuel 24.1–17
Pentecost 11	Isaiah 42.1–12	1 Chronicles 29.1–16
Pentecost 12	Isaiah 49.1–13	stet
Pentecost 13	Isaiah 50.4–11	Jeremiah 11.18–20, 12.1–6
Pentecost 14	Leviticus 19.1–4, 9–18	Deuteronomy 15.1–18
Pentecost 15	Isaiah 54.1–17	Genesis 45.1–28
Pentecost 16	Isaiah 45.1–13	stet
Pentecost 17	Jeremiah 7.1–14	Jeremiah 32.1–15
Pentecost 18	Deuteronomy 26.1–11, 16–19	Ecclesiasticus 38.24–34 *or* Nehemiah 6.1–16
Pentecost 19	stet	Daniel 6.1–23
Pentecost 20	stet	Isaiah 33.13–22
Pentecost 21	Daniel 3.1–25	Genesis 32.1–30

APPENDIX I

INDEX OF SCRIPTURE PASSAGES USED

	1st Year	*2nd Year*
Genesis	1.1–3, 24–31a	2.4b–9, 15–25
	3.1–15	4.1–10
	8.13–22	9.9–17
	12.1–9	22.1–18
	28.10–22	32.24–30
		45.1–15
Exodus	3.1–15	6.2–8
	12.1–11	12.1–11
	14.15–22	14.15–22
	15.1–11	16.4–15
	19.1–6	
	20.1–17	
	24.3–8	
	33.12–23	
	34.29–35	
Leviticus	19.9–18	
Deuteronomy	6.17–25	6.4–9
	7.6–9a	6.10–17
	8.1–6	8.11–20
	26.1–11	10.12–11.1
	30.15–20	15.7–11
		16.1–6
		34.1–12
Joshua	1.1–9	24.14–25
Ruth		1.8–17, 22
1 Samuel	1.20–28	3.1–10
	16.1–13	17.37–50
		24.9–17
2 Samuel		7.4–16

	1st Year	*2nd Year*
1 Kings		3.5–15
		8.22–30
		10.1–13
		17.17–24
		19.1–12
2 Kings	6.8–17	2.1–15
		5.1–14
1 Chronicles		29.1–9
Nehemiah		6.1–16
Job	42.1–6	
Proverbs		3.1–8
		4.10–18
Isaiah	6.1–8	9.2–7
	9.2–7	12.1–6
	11.1–9	33.17–22
	12.1–6	35.1–10
	25.6–9	42.1–7
	30.18–21	45.18–25
	40.1–11	49.7–13
	42.1–7	51.4–11
	45.1–7	52.13 – 53.12
	49.1–6	64.1–5
	50.4–9	
	51.1–6	
	52.1–10	
	54.1–8	
	55.1–11	
	58.1–8	
	59.15–20	
	60.1–6	
	61.1–3	
	62.1–5	
	63.1–9	
Jeremiah	1.4–10	12.1–6
	7.1–7	31.31–34
	29.1, 4–14	32.6–15
Ezekiel	36.24–28	34.7–15
		37.1–14

	1st Year	*2nd Year*
Daniel	3.13–25	6.10–23
	7.9–14	7.13–14
	7.13–14	
Hosea	11.1–9	
	14.1–7	
Joel	2.23–29	2.28–32
Amos		5.6–15
Jonah		1.1–17
Micah	5.2–4	4.1–7
		5.2–4
		6.1–8
Zephaniah	3.14–20	
Zechariah	9.9–12	2.10–13
Malachi		3.1–5
Ecclesiasticus		38.24–34
Matthew	2.1–12	1.18–23
	3.13–17	2.1–12
	4.1–17	5.13–16
	5.1–12	10.16–22
	5.21–26	11.2–15
	6.16–21	11.25–30
	7.21–29	12.22–32
	16.13–28	21.1–11
	17.1–8	24.34–46
	18.21–35	25.1–13
	19.16–26	25.14–29
	22.15–22	25.31–46
	28.16–20	28.1–10
		28.16–20
Mark	1.14–20	1.35–45
	2.1–12	4.35–41
	2.13–17	7.14–23
	10.2–16	9.14–29
	11.1–11	10.32–45
	16.1–8	10.46–52
		12.28–34
		13.5–13

	1st Year	*2nd Year*
Luke	1.26–38	2.1–20
	2.1–20	2.41–52
	2.21–40	4.1–13
	5.1–11	4.14–21
	9.51–62	6.27–38
	10.25–37	7.1–10
	11.14–26	7.36–50
	12.1–7	8.4–15
	15.11–32	8.41–55
	21.25–33	9.18–27
	24.13–35	9.28–36
	24.44–53	11.1–13
		12.22–31
		14.15–24
		14.25–33
		15.1–10
		16.19–31
		17.5–10
		17.11–19
		18.9–14
		19.1–10
		20.9–16
		24.44–53
John	1.1–14(twice)	1.1–14
	1.19–27	1.29–34
	2.1–11	1.35–51
	3.13–21	2.13–22
	5.36–47	3.1–8
	6.1–14	4.7–14
	6.27–35	6.35–40
	8.51–58	10.7–18
	12.20–32	11.17–27
	13.1–15	14.1–11
	13.33–36	14.15–27
	14.8–17	16.12–24
	14.15–27	(18&)19.1–37
	15.1–5	20.1–18
	15.6–11	

	1st Year	2nd Year
John	15.12–15	
	15.16–27	
	16.1–11	
	16.25–33	
	17.1–10	
	17.11–19	
	17.20–26	
	(18&)19.1–37	
	20.1–18	
	20.19–29	
	21.1–14	
	21.15–22	
Acts	1.1–11	1.1–11
	2.1–11	2.1–11
	10.34–48	2.22–24, 32–36
	26.1, 9–18	2.37–47
		4.5–12
		8.26–38
		11.4–18
		17.22–31
		20.17–35
Romans	3.21–26	5.1–11
	4.13–25	8.1–11
	6.1–11	8.12–17
	7.7–12	8.18–25
	12.1–8	8.28–39
	12.9–21	13.8–14
	13.1–7	
	15.4–13	
1 Corinthians	1.18–25	2.1–10
	1.26–31	3.10–17
	4.1–5	5.7b–8
	4.8–13	9.19–27
	9.24–27	12.4–13
	13.1–13	15.12–20
	15.1–11	15.53–58
	15.12–20	
	15.21–28	

	1st Year	2nd Year
2 Corinthians	3.12–18	4.11–18
	4.1–10	6.1–10
	5.14–21	12.1–10
	8.1–9	
Galatians	3.26–4.7	1.11–24
	5.16–25	2.20–3.9
		6.1–10
Ephesians	1.3–14	2.1–10
	1.15–23	3.1–6
	5.1–10	3.8–19
	5.21 – 6.4	4.1–8, 11–13
	6.10–18a	4.17–32
Philippians	2.1–13	1.1–11
	3.7–21	4.4–9
	4.10–20	
Colossians	1.15–20	1.24–29
	2.8–15	3.1–11
	3.12–17	
1 Thessalonians	5.1–11	
1 Timothy		2.1–7
2 Timothy		3.14 – 4.5
Titus	2.11–15	2.11–15
Philemon	1–16	
Hebrews	1.1–4	4.12–16
	2.14–18	9.11–15
	3.1–6	10.1–10
	10.11–25	10.11–25
	11.1–3, 7–16	11.17–29
	11.32 – 12.2	
James	1.22–27	1.2–12
	5.13–16	2.14–24
		4.1–8a
1 Peter	1.3–9	3.1–9
	2.1–10	4.7–11
	2.19–25	5.1–11
	4.12–19	
2 Peter		1.16–19

	1st Year	*2nd Year*
1 John	1.1–4	3.1–8
	4.1–6	3.9–18
	4.7–14	4.7–14
		4.15–21
Revelation	1.12–18	4.1–11
	3.14–22	7.9–17
	19.6–9	21.1–7

APPENDIX II

	1st Year	2nd Year	Total	Verses used more than once
Genesis	58	77	135	
Exodus	93	38	131	19
Leviticus	10	—	10	
Deuteronomy	36	59	95	1
Joshua	9	12	21	
Ruth	—	11	11	
1 Samuel	22	33	55	
2 Samuel	—	13	13	
1 Kings	—	53	53	
2 Kings	10	29	39	
1 Chronicles	—	9	9	
Nehemiah	—	16	16	
Job	6	—	6	
Proverbs	—	17	17	
Isaiah	146	78	224	22
Jeremiah	26	20	46	
Ezekiel	5	23	28	
Daniel	21	16	37	4
Hosea	16	—	16	
Joel	7	5	12	2
Amos	—	10	10	
Jonah	—	17	17	
Micah	3	18	21	3
Zephaniah	7	—	7	
Zechariah	4	4	8	
Malachi	—	5	5	
	479	563	1042	51

	1st Year	2nd Year	Total	Verses used more than once
Ecclesiasticus	—	11	11	
Matthew	130	144	274	17
Mark	58	81	139	
Luke	173	250	423	30
John	318	184	502	101
Acts	48	106	154	22
Romans	74	55	129	
1 Corinthians	70	54	124	13
2 Corinthians	34	28	62	
Galatians	21	35	56	
Ephesians	57	55	112	
Philippians	39	17	56	
Colossians	20	17	37	
1 Thessalonians	11	—	11	
1 Timothy	—	7	7	
2 Timothy	—	8	8	
Titus	5	5	10	5
Philemon	16	—	16	
Hebrews	54	48	102	15
James	10	30	40	
1 Peter	32	25	57	
2 Peter	—	4	4	
1 John	18	33	51	8
Revelation	20	27	47	
New Testament	1208	1213	2421	211
Old Testament	479	563	1042	51
Apocrypha		11	11	
	1687	1787	3474	262
Verses used more than once			262	
Number of different verses used			3212	

APPENDIX III

Total Number of Verses Used

	1st Year	2nd Year
9th before Christmas	31	36
8th before Christmas	30	30
7th before Christmas	23	28
6th before Christmas	30	37
5th before Christmas	30	29
4th before Christmas	30	31
3rd before Christmas	33	21
2nd before Christmas	25	25
1st before Christmas	28	17
Christmas Day (i)	28	28
(ii)	28	28
Christmas 1	22	25
Christmas 2	37	24
Christmas 3	33	23
Christmas 4	25	41
Christmas 5	27	27
Christmas 6	28	33
9th before Easter	22	30
8th before Easter	23	35
7th before Easter	31	35
Ash Wednesday	18	24
6th before Easter	28	26
5th before Easter	29	29
4th before Easter	29	24
3rd before Easter	22	25
2nd before Easter	30	23
1st before Easter	23	36
Good Friday	63	63
Easter Day (i)	21	18
(ii)	35	35

	1st Year	*2nd Year*
Easter 1	29	24
Easter 2	31	32
Easter 3	28	30
Easter 4	22	28
Easter 5	23	37
Ascension Day	18	18
Easter 6	25	36
Pentecost	31	29
Pentecost 1	30	20
Pentecost 2	21	34
Pentecost 3	26	33
Pentecost 4	19	35
Pentecost 5	38	35
Pentecost 6	34	31
Pentecost 7	37	30
Pentecost 8	27	36
Pentecost 9	27	40
Pentecost 10	34	34
Pentecost 11	23	26
Pentecost 12	21	21
Pentecost 13	25	32
Pentecost 14	36	25
Pentecost 15	40	33
Pentecost 16	22	31
Pentecost 17	22	31
Pentecost 18	26	★32
Pentecost 19	37	35
Pentecost 20	37	28
Pentecost 21	36	29
	1687	1771 16★
	1687	1787

★16 alternative lection